Color Coastal Art

VOLUME I

30 COASTAL INSPIRED HAND DRAWN DESIGNS

JEANO ROBERTS

ISBN-13: 978-1518811319
ISBN-10: 1518811310

COLOR COASTAL ART
ADULT COLORING BOOKS AND PAGES WITH A BEACH THEME

Jeano Roberts ~ Artist

Do you love the beach? All things coastal and tropical?

Well this coloring book is for you!

Let me share a little about myself...

Always been an artist and grew up in Cocoa Beach Florida. I love creating coastal themed art. Years of surfing and bird watching enable me to create images of what I am familiar with. I am so exciting to be able to create these fun coloring images for you to relax with and enjoy filling with bright or soft colors, you choose!

All of my coloring pages are hand-drawn. I use pencil first then use ink for the finished appearance. You will find areas that are not perfect~ hence the nature of hand-drawn art. But your coloring results will be lovely.

Color these while on your Beach Vacation or when home to bring you back to those wonderful relaxing moments.

- use the blotter pages to protect the following page and get tips!

- Be sure to sign up for my mailing list ~ http://ColorCoastalArt.com. I will be using this list to stay in contact to let you know about my upcoming books and to get feed back from you!

- I want to create books and pages you enjoy coloring so let me know what you like and what you would like to have me create for your coloring pleasure.

Enjoy your coloring pages and if you have ANY questions, don't hesitate to ask me!

JEAN

Extra sheet for use as a Blotter

AND COLOR TESTER!

Tip: opposite colors on the color wheel create nice shaded areas. Don't just use black or gray.   (print out or pick up a color wheel)

Example: Try using green on top of the red to create a shadowed edge on an object like an apple!

Experiment here first ☺

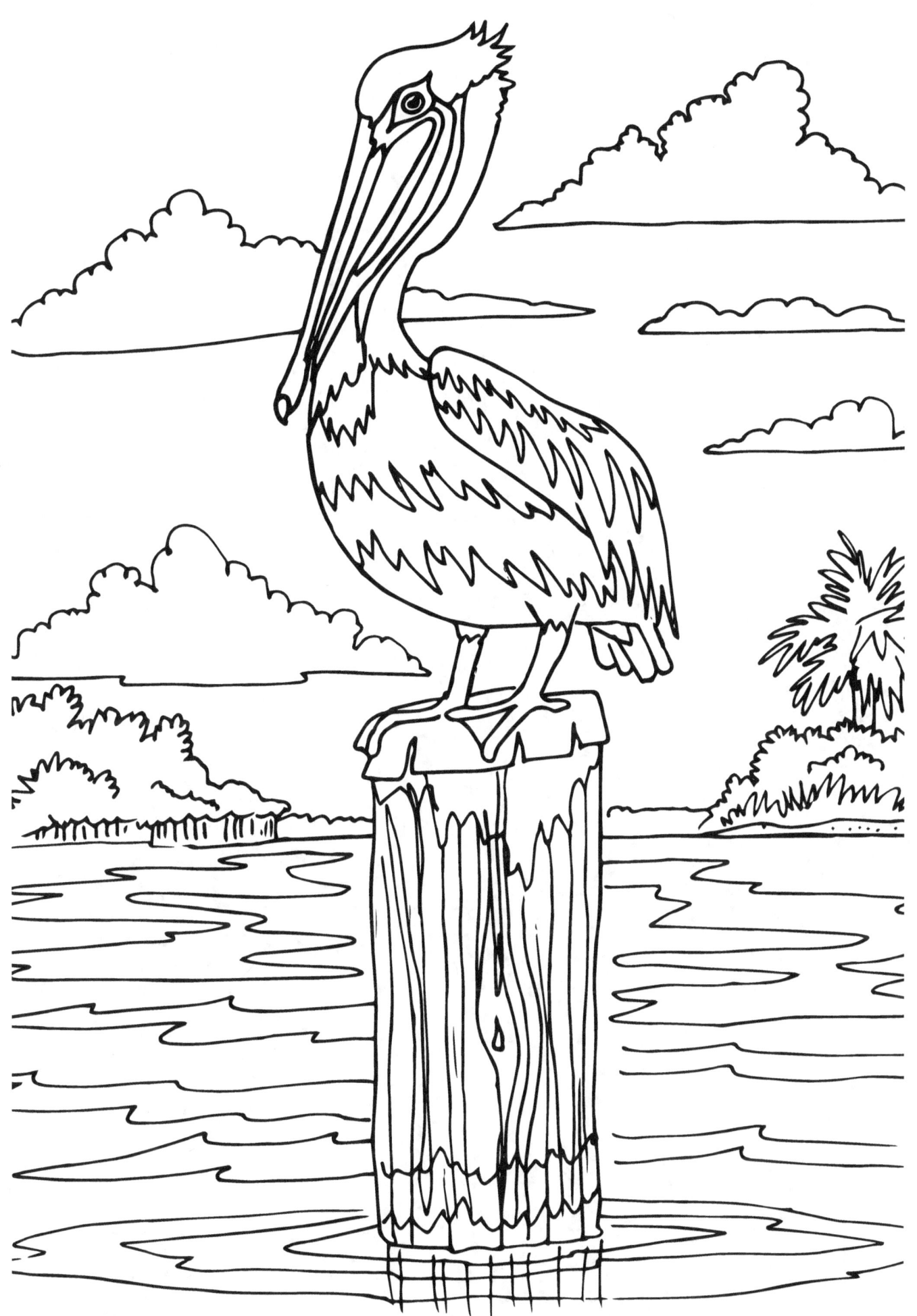

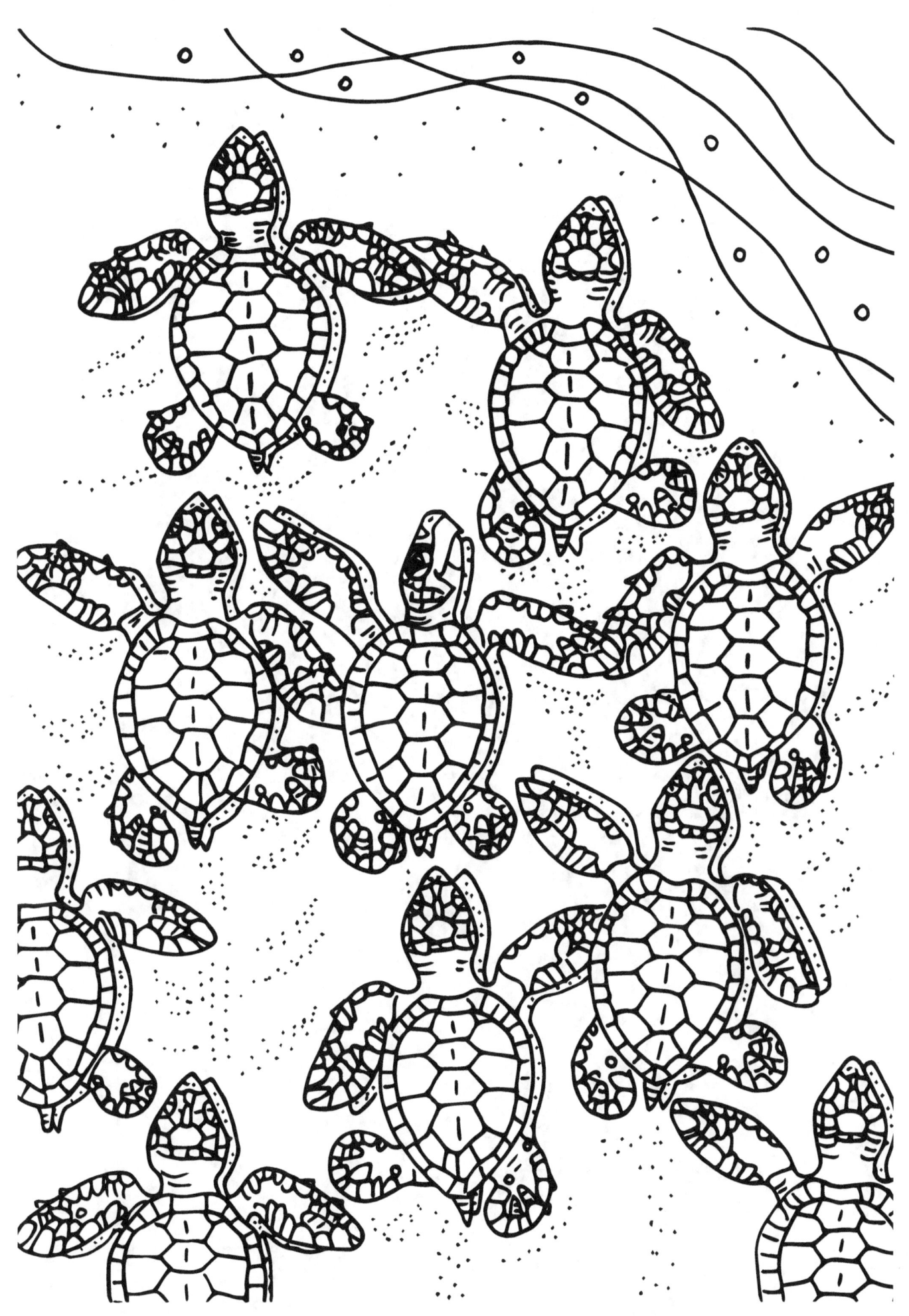

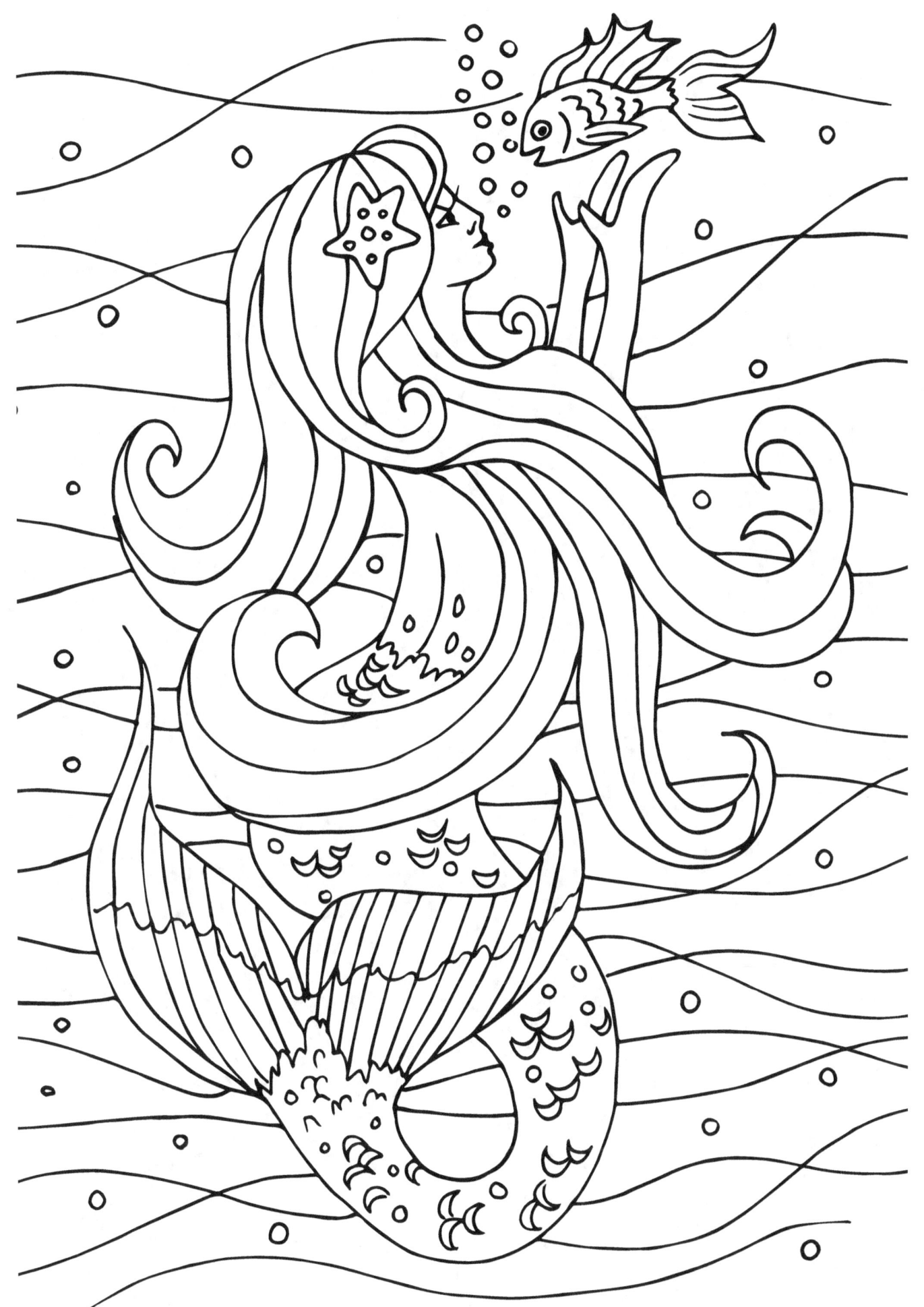

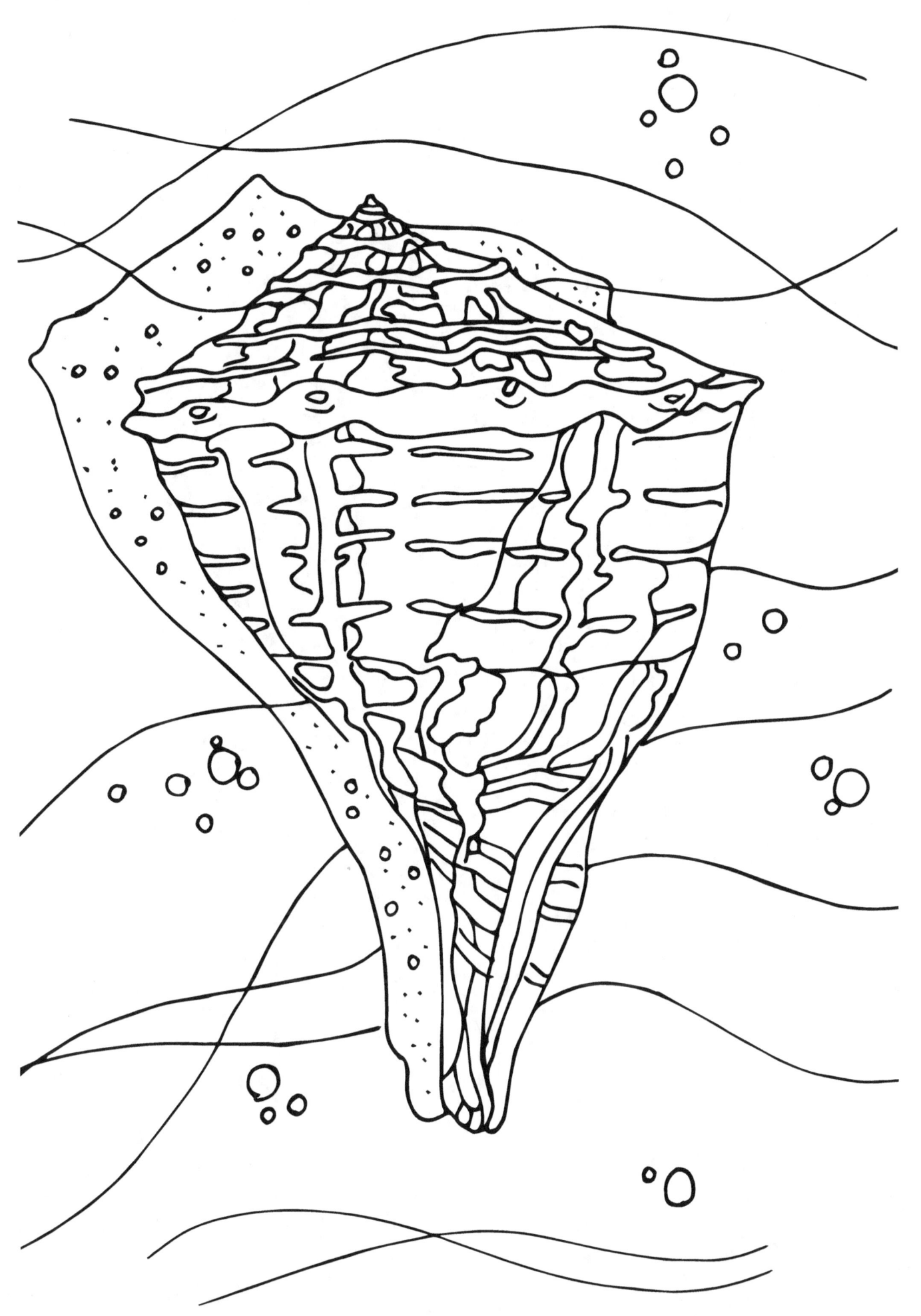

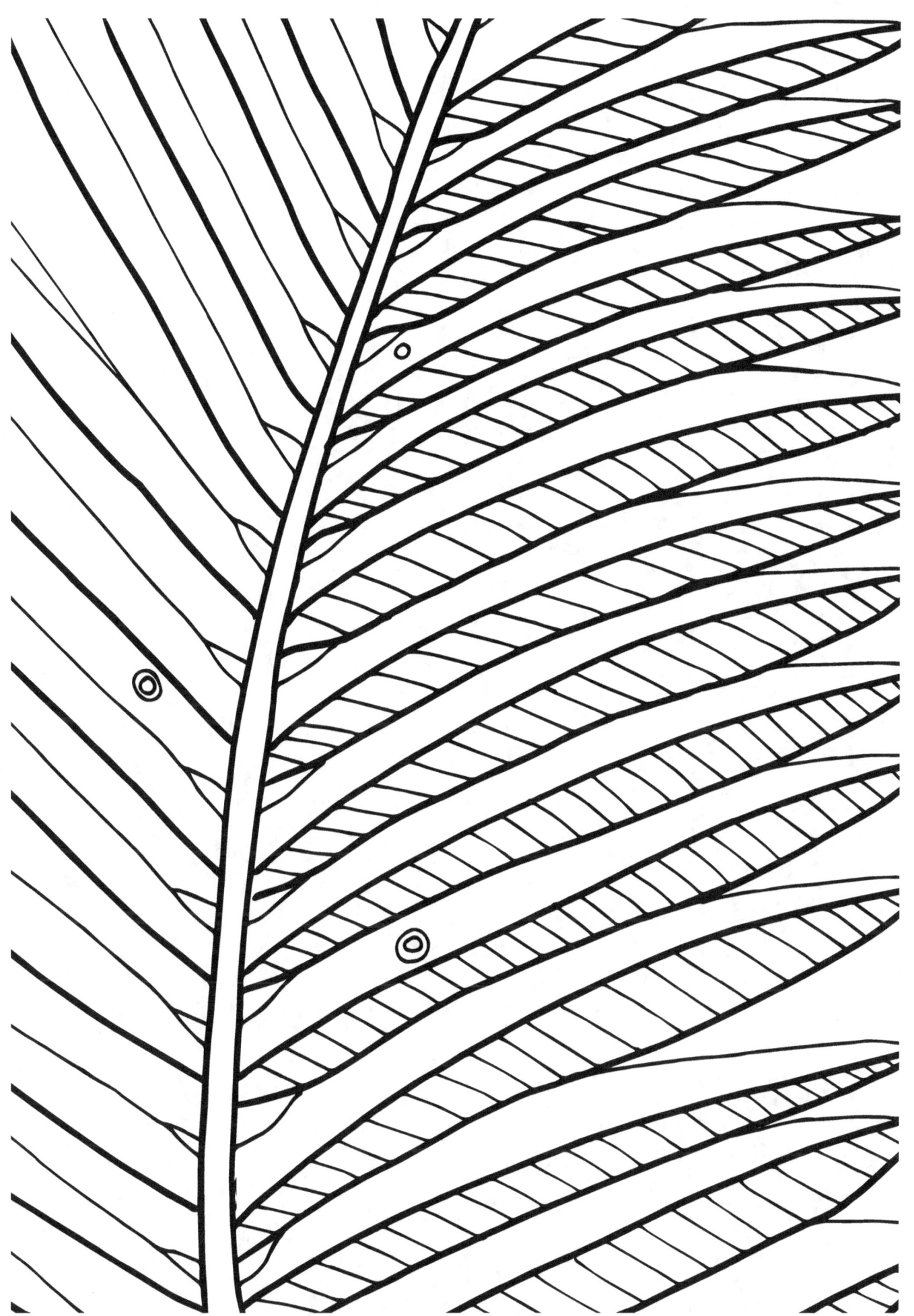

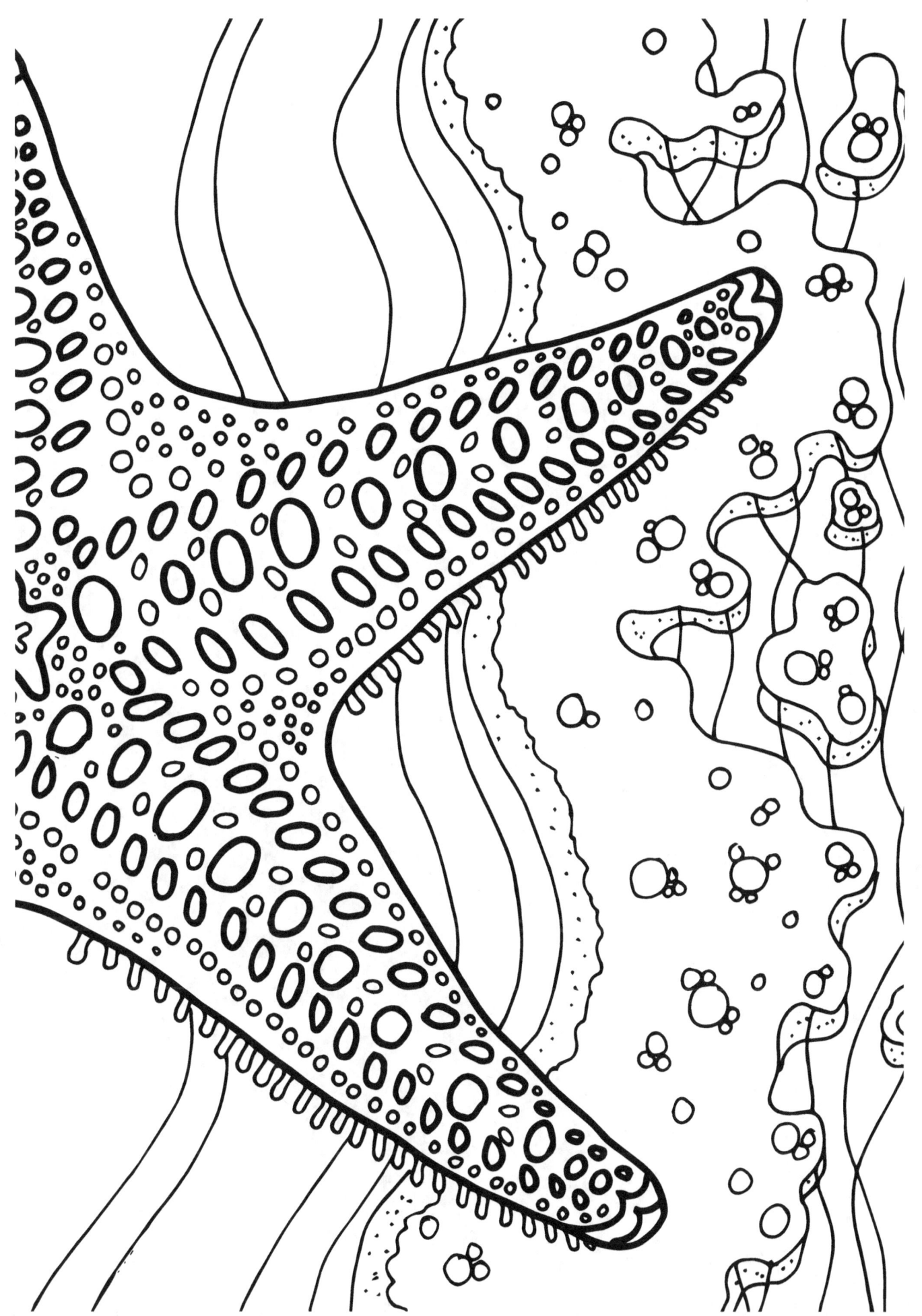

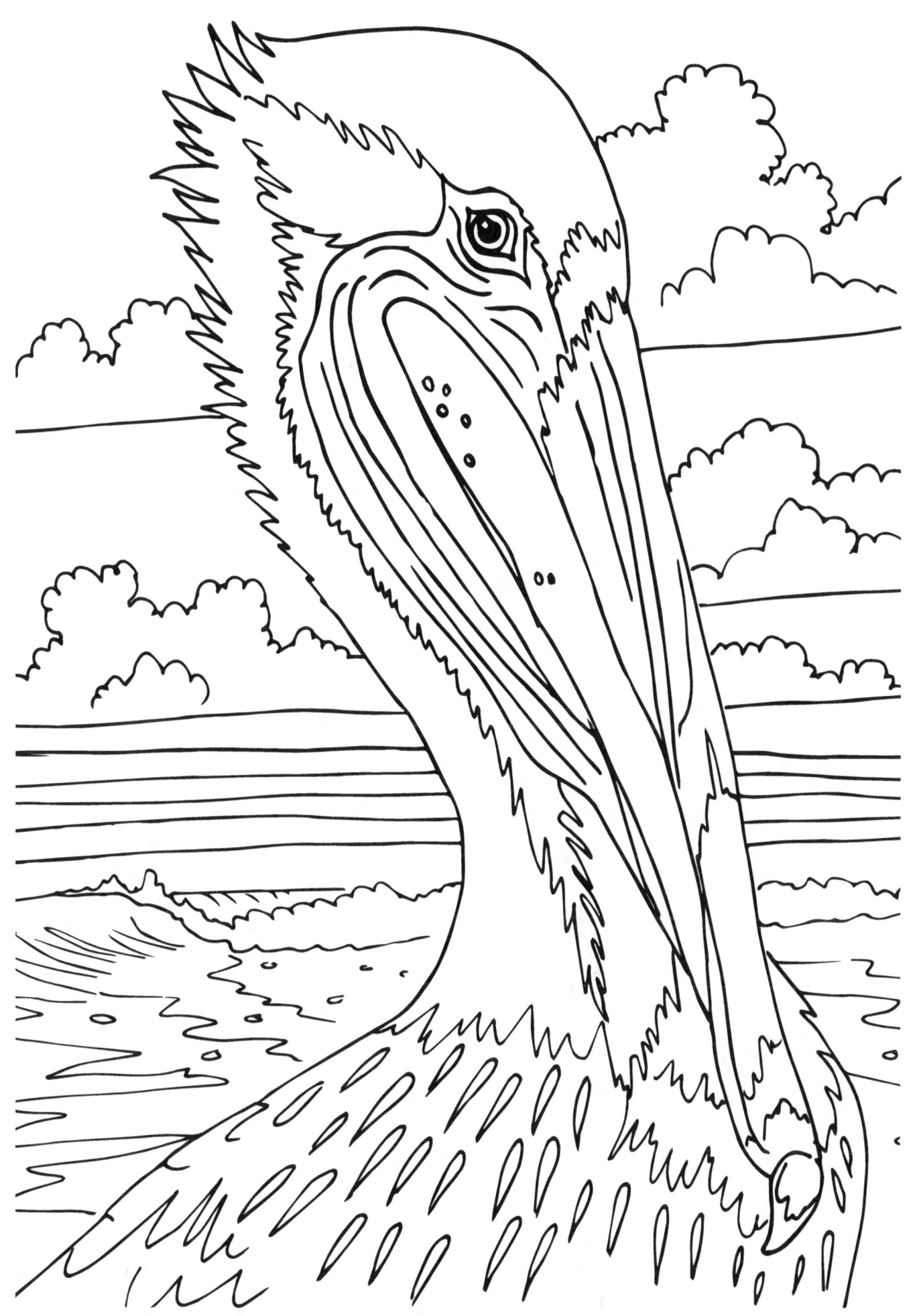

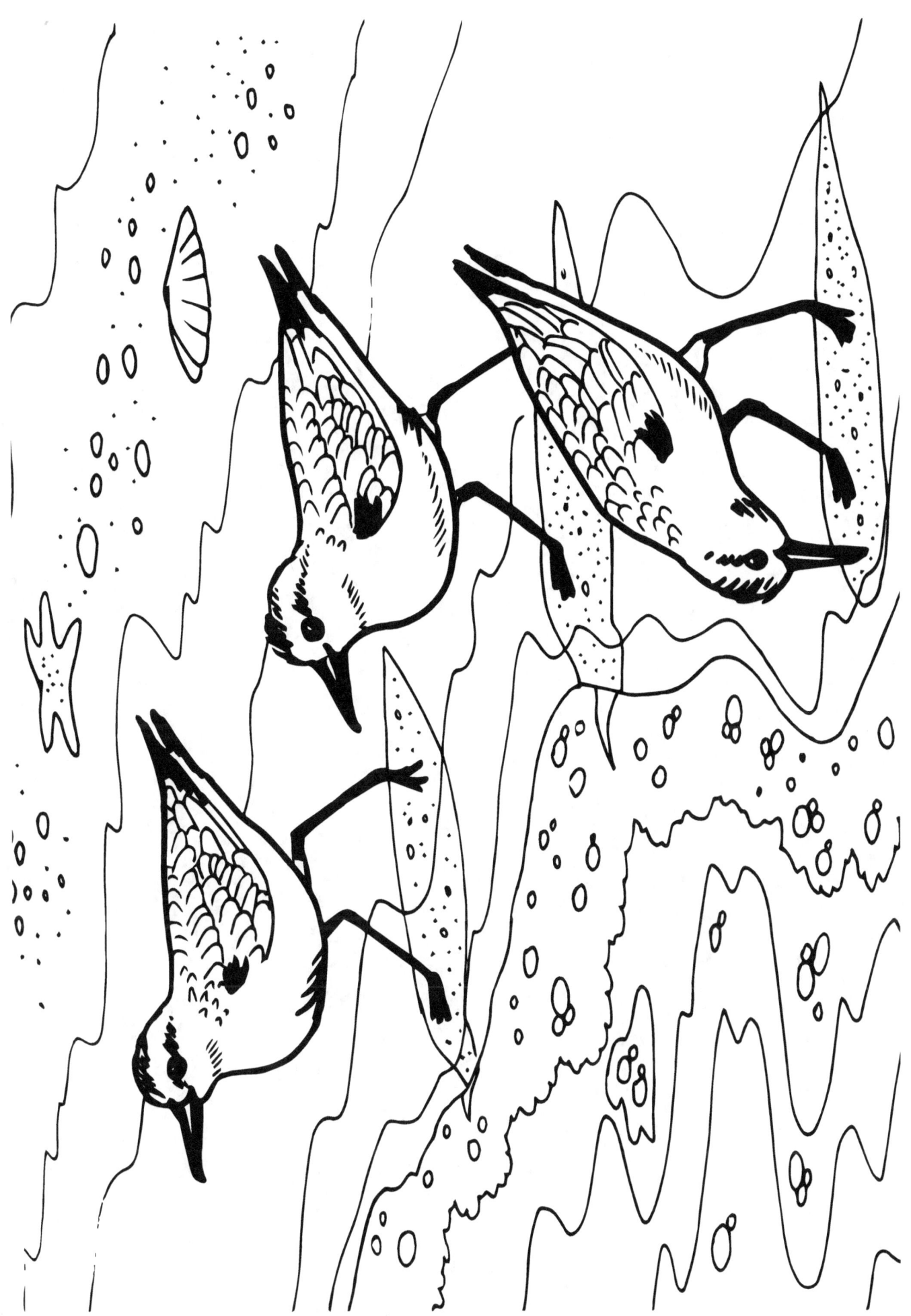

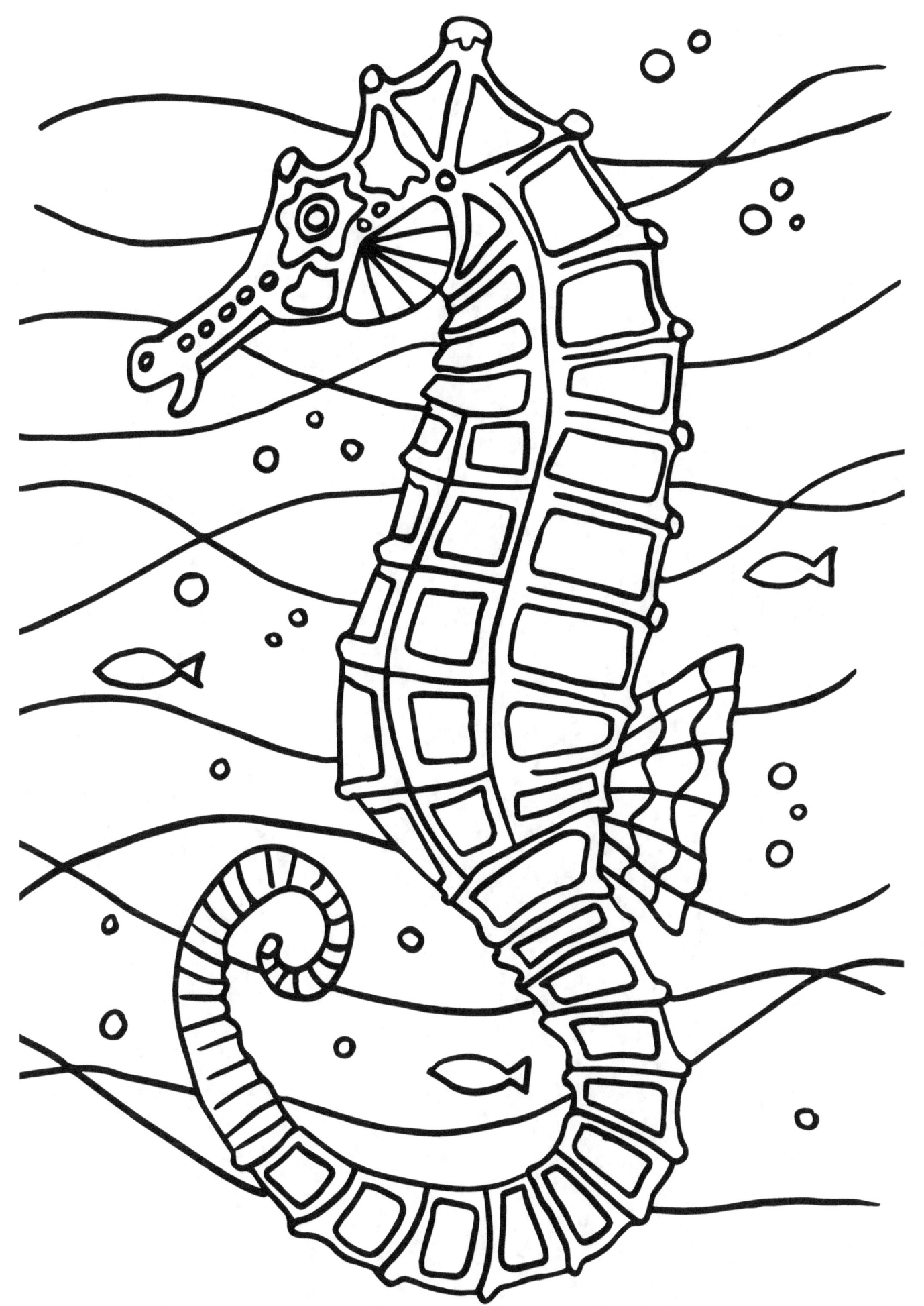

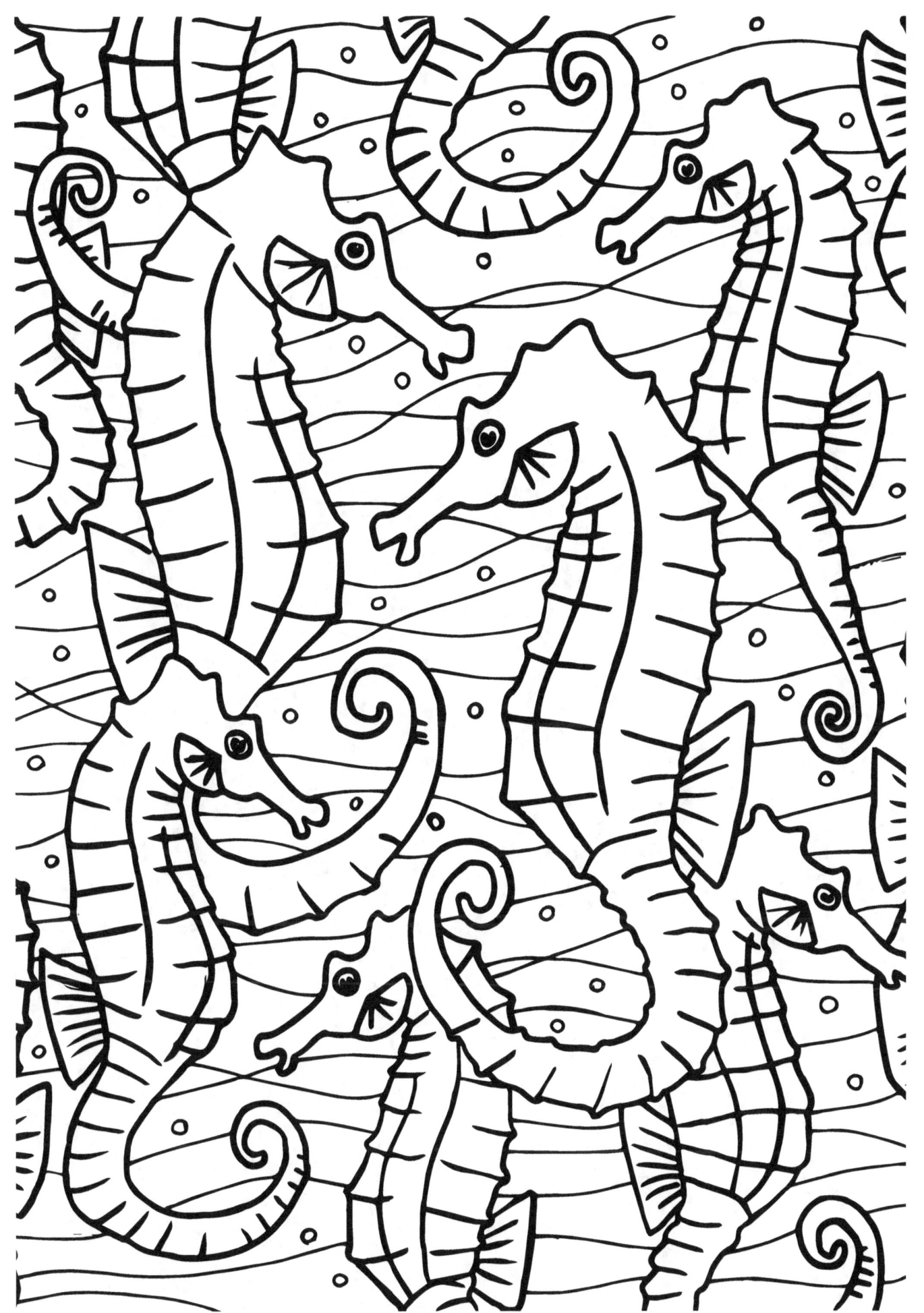

Extra sheet
for use as a
Blotter

AND COLOR TESTER!

Tip: Always make copies of your pages before you color so you can color them over and over again!

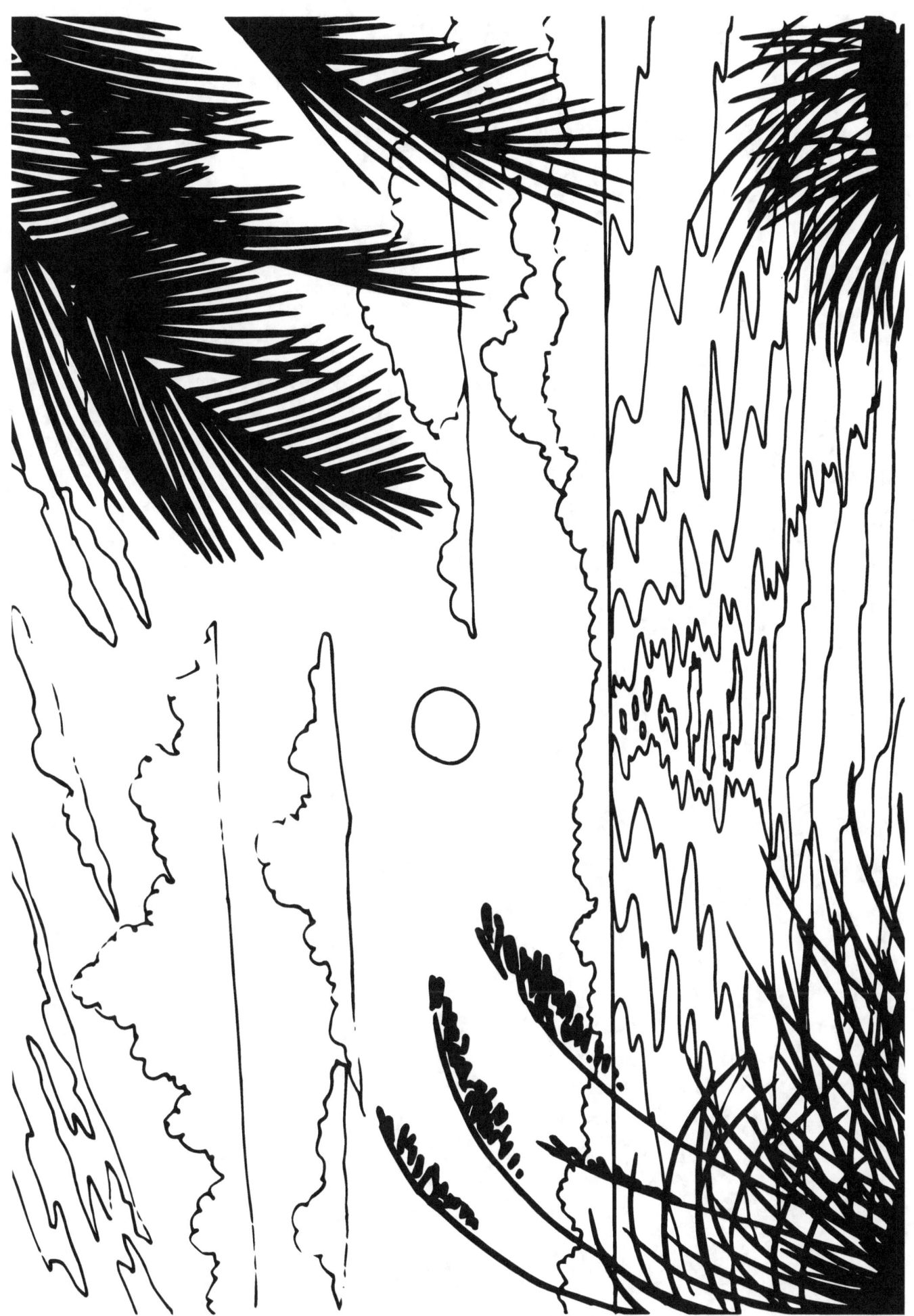

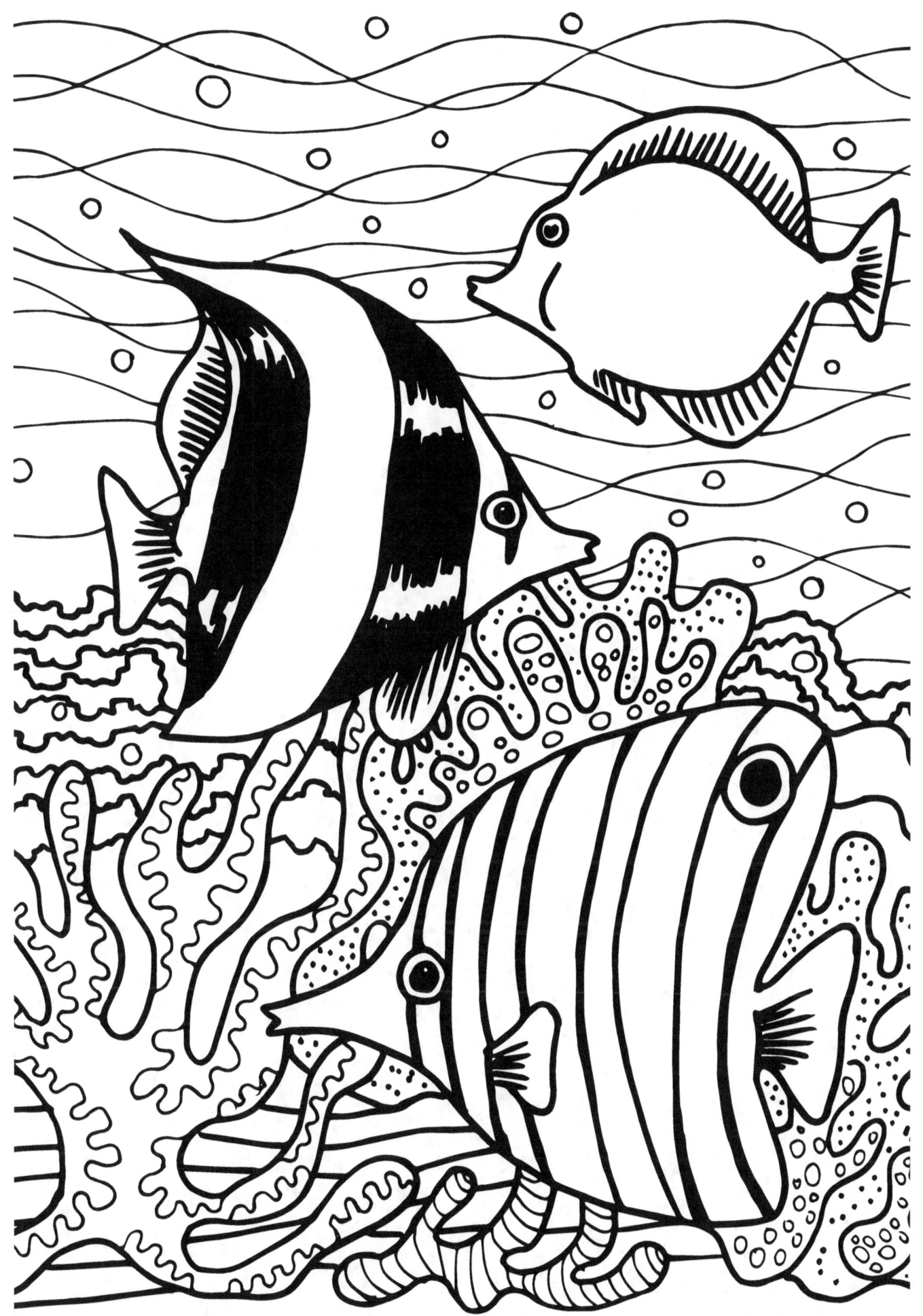

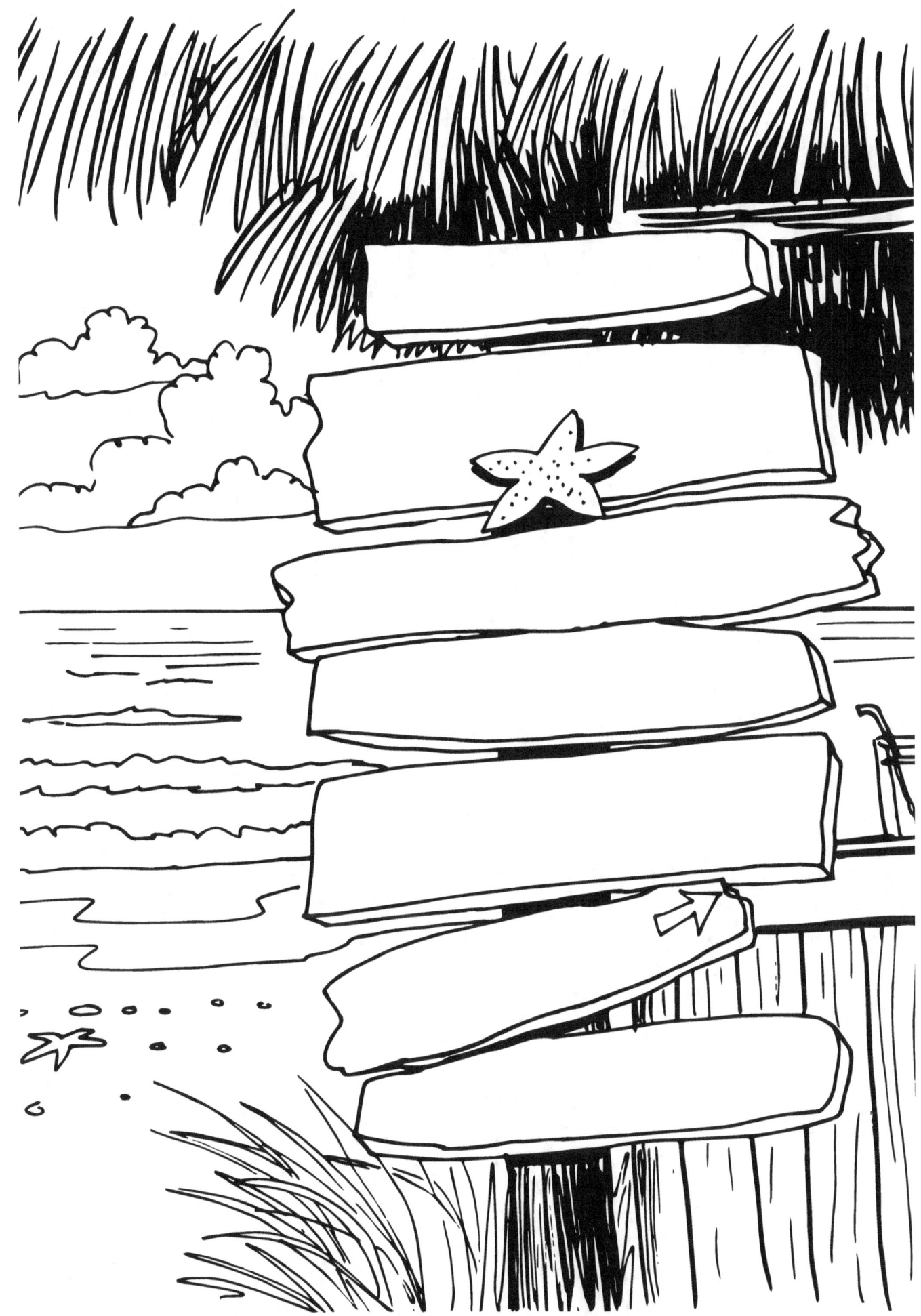

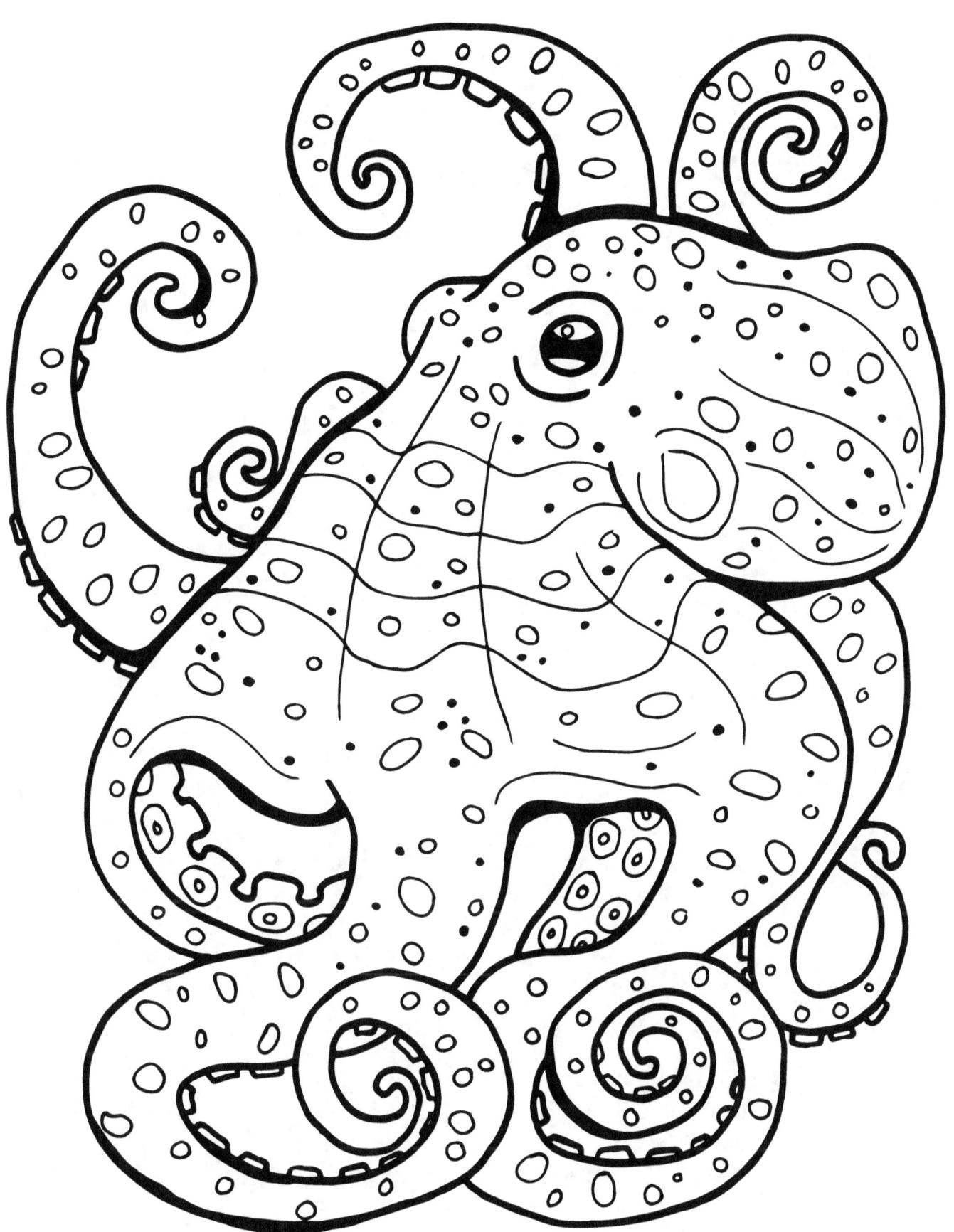

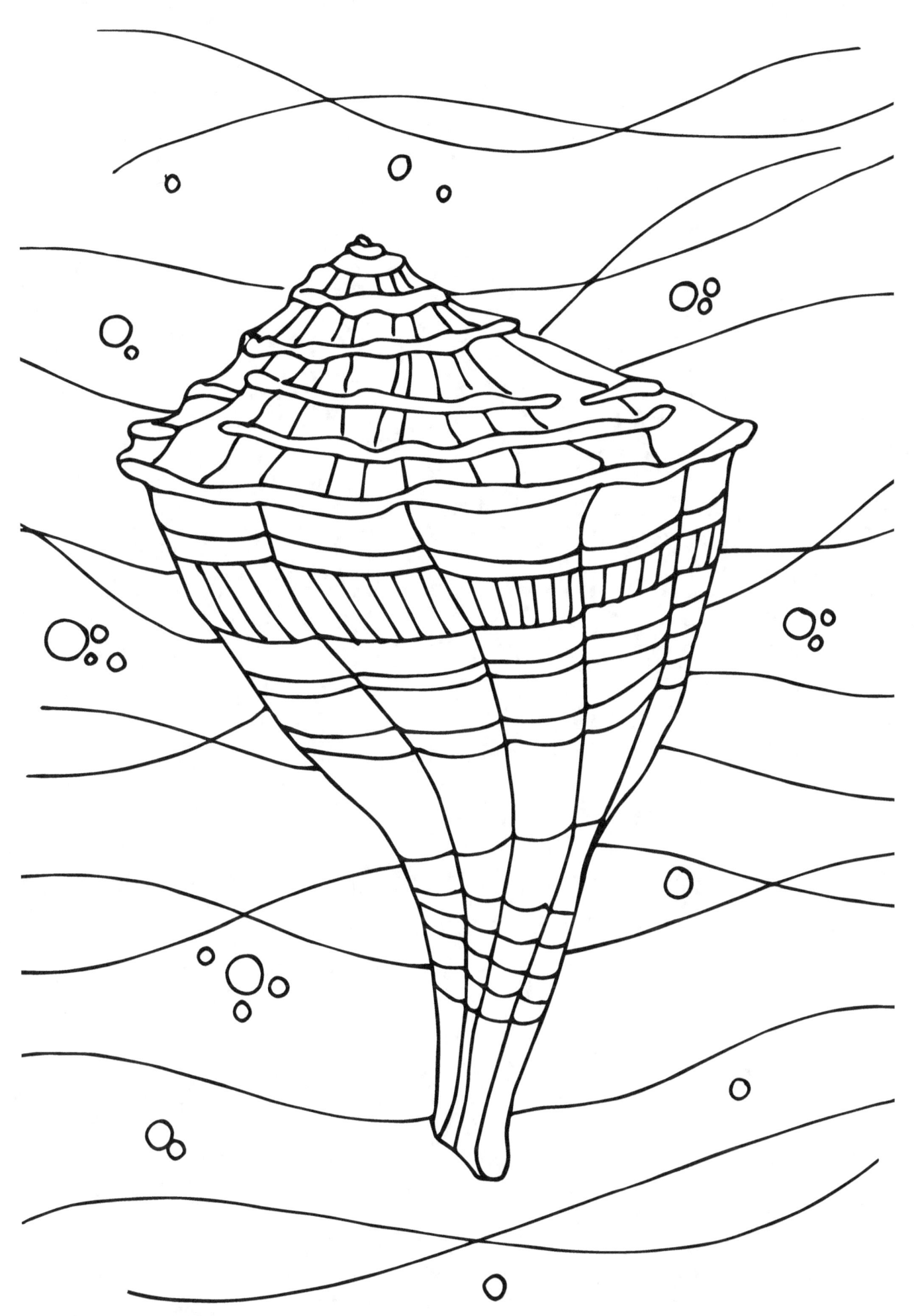

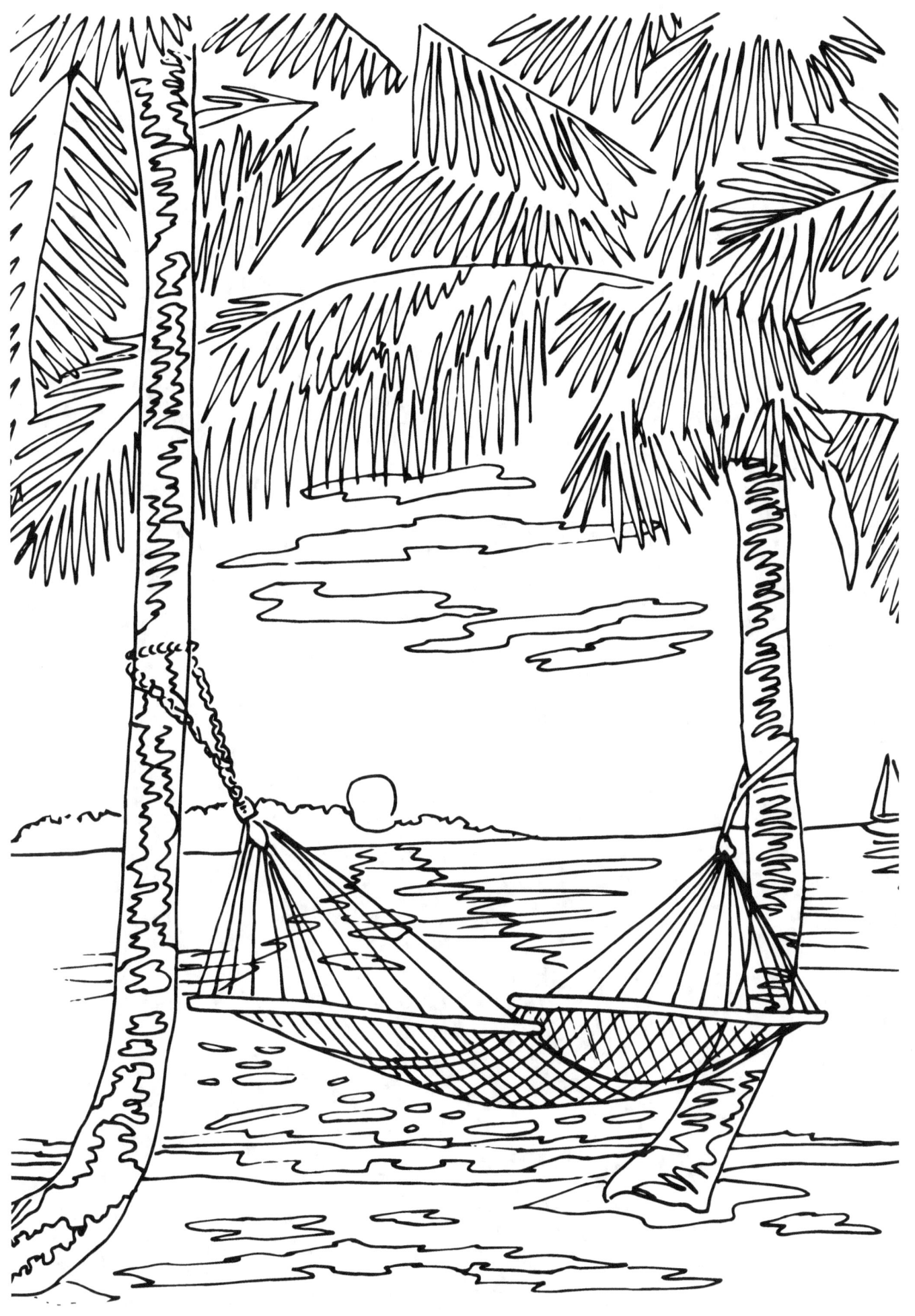

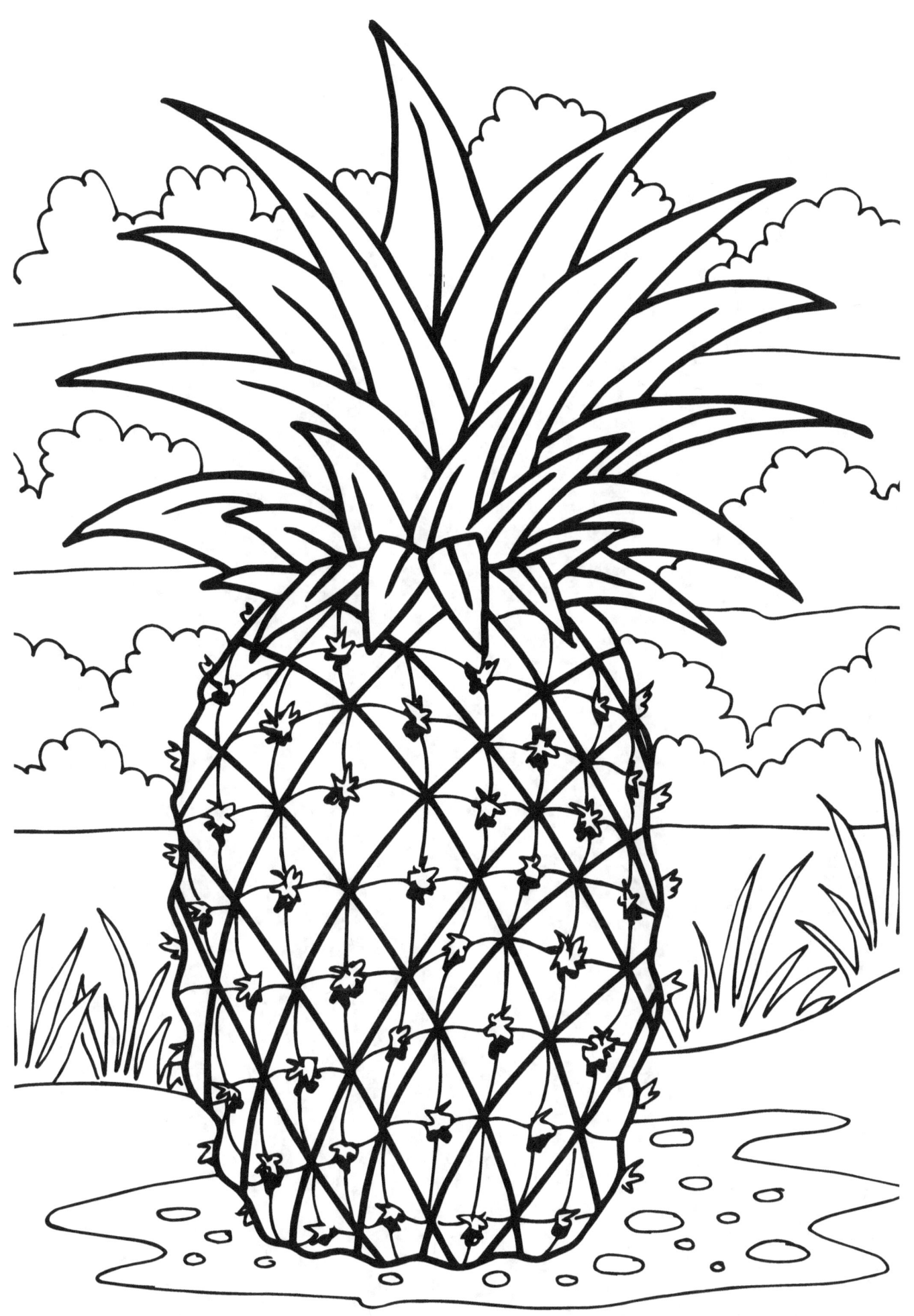

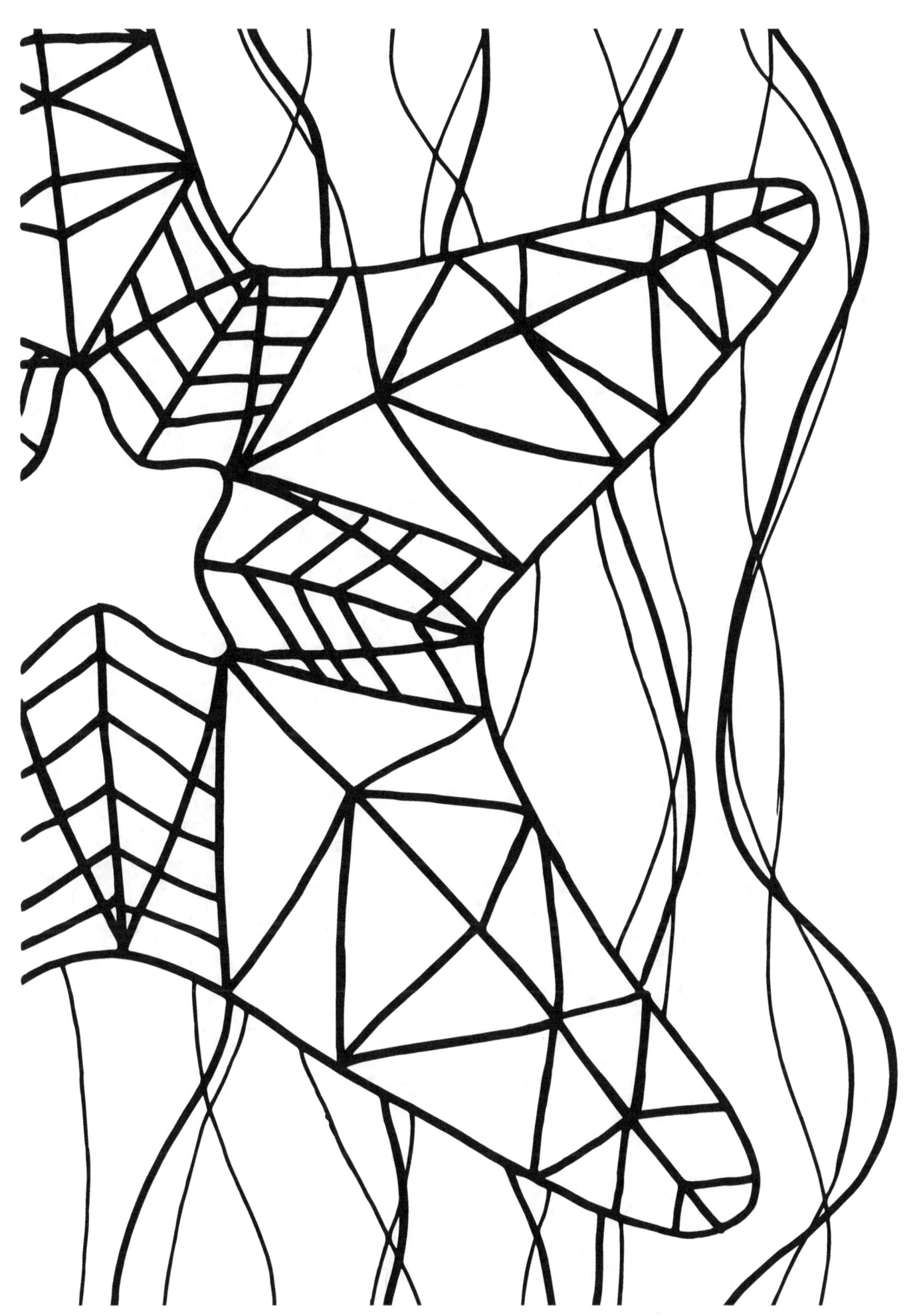

Extra sheet
for use as a
Blotter

AND COLOR TESTER!

Tip: try layering colors to
create new ones!
Example: yellow and pink or
red can make a nice orange!

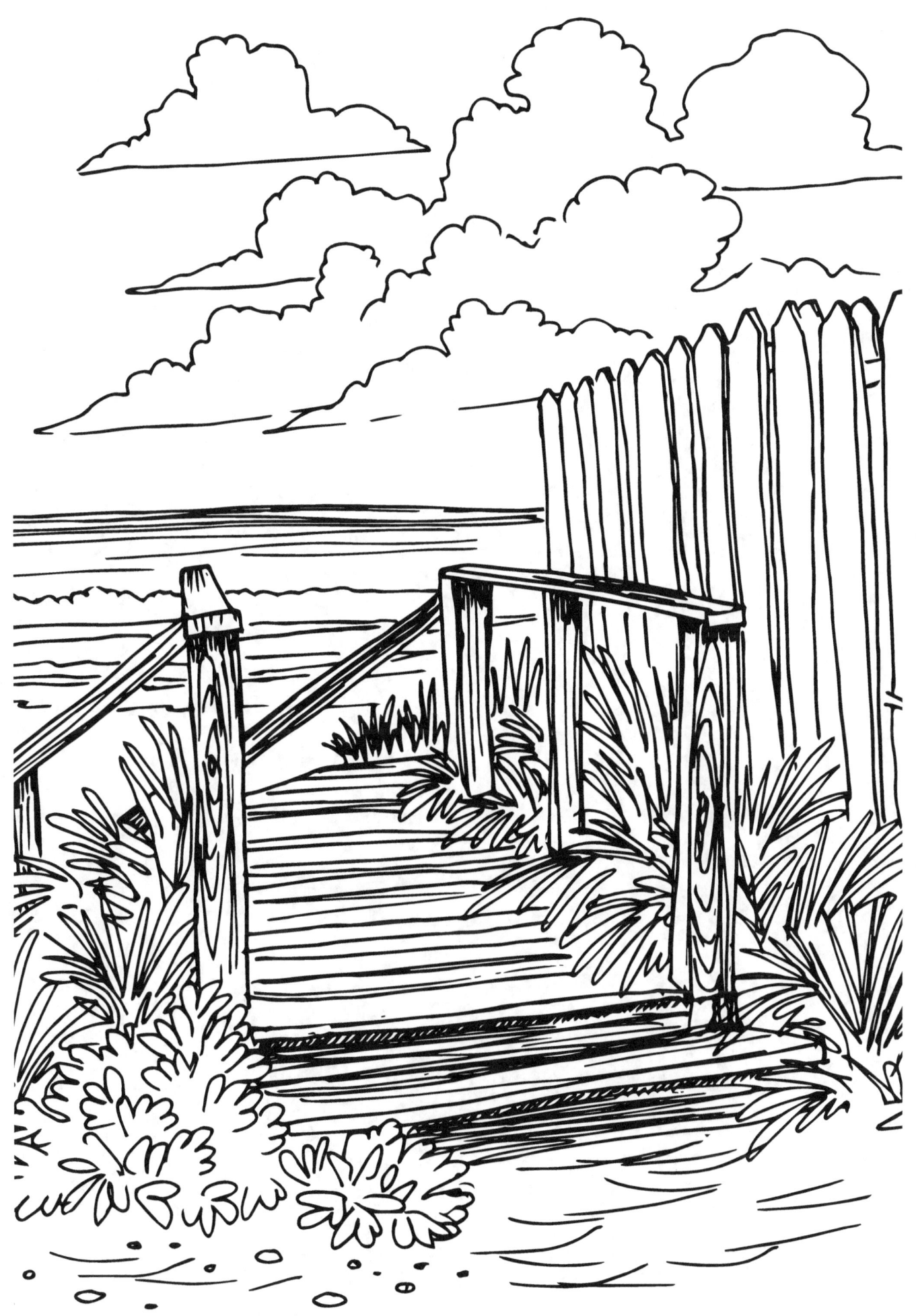

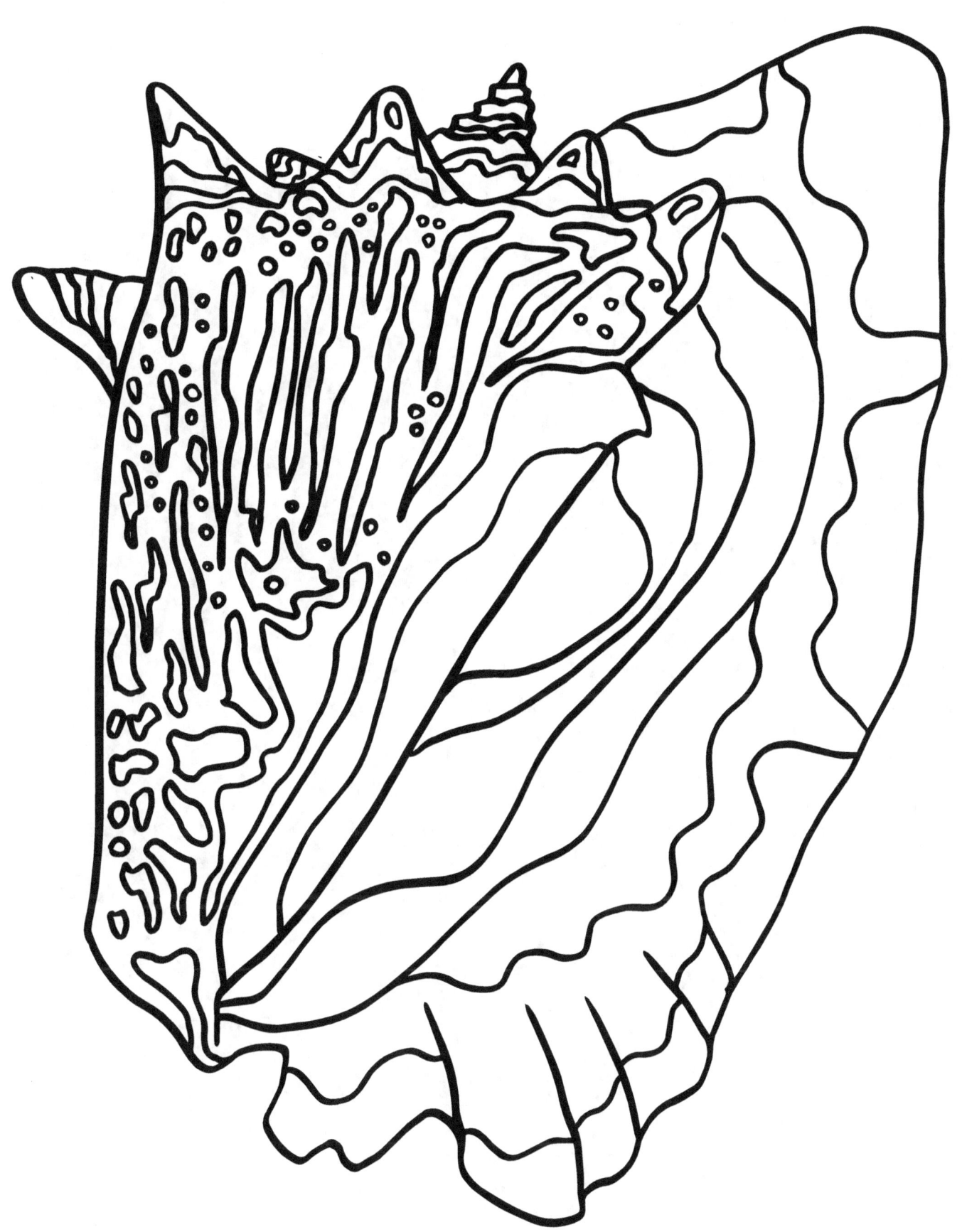

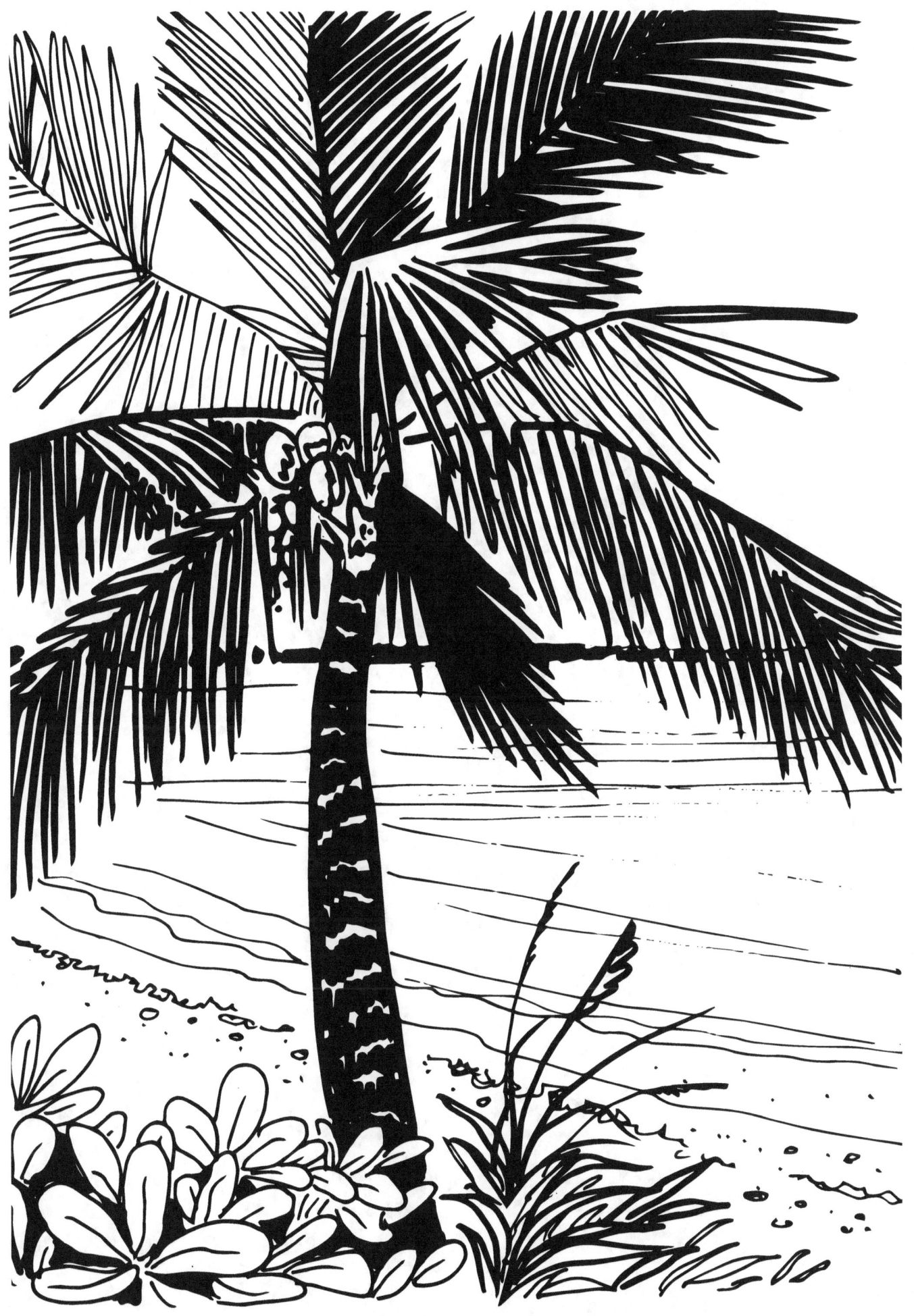

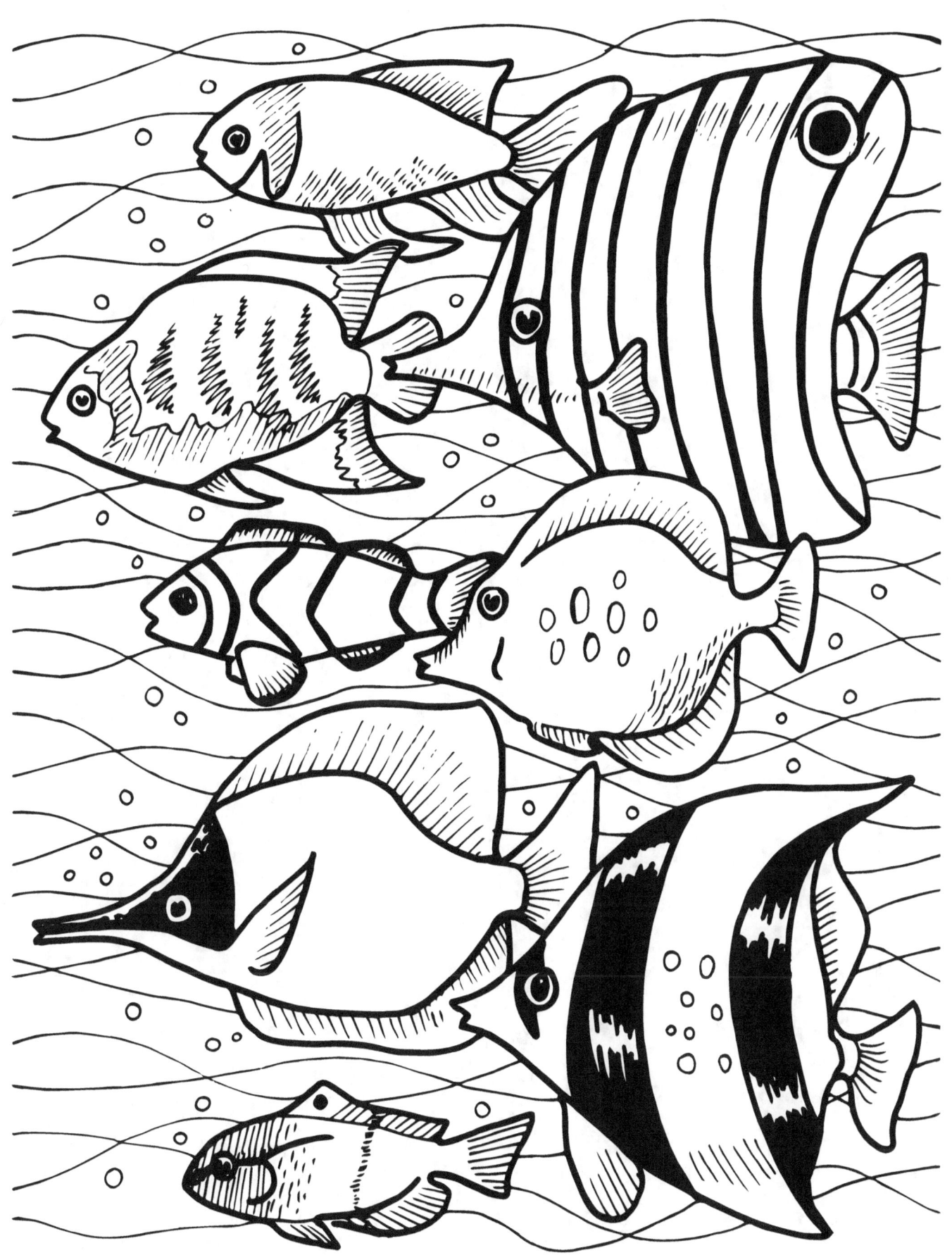

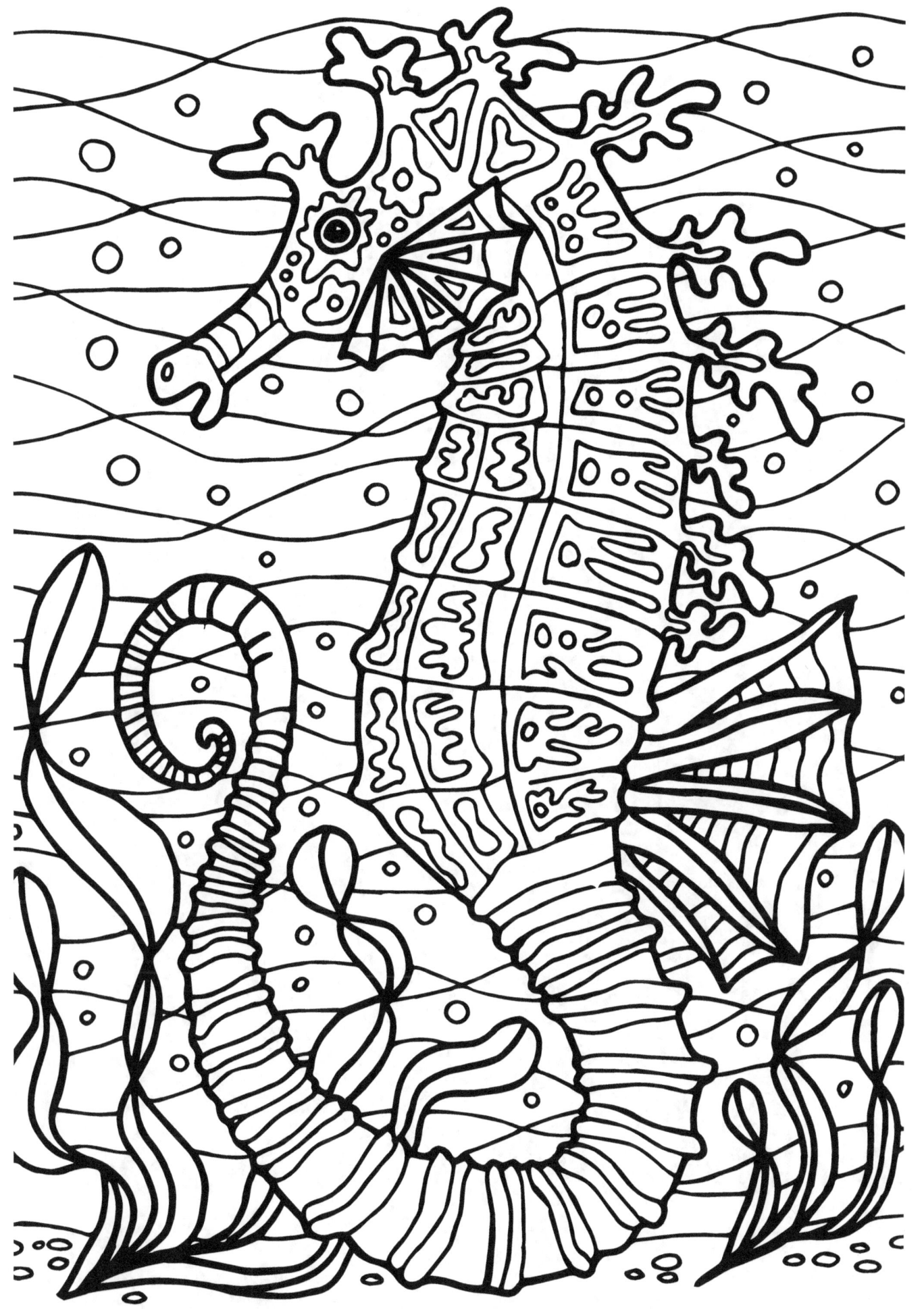

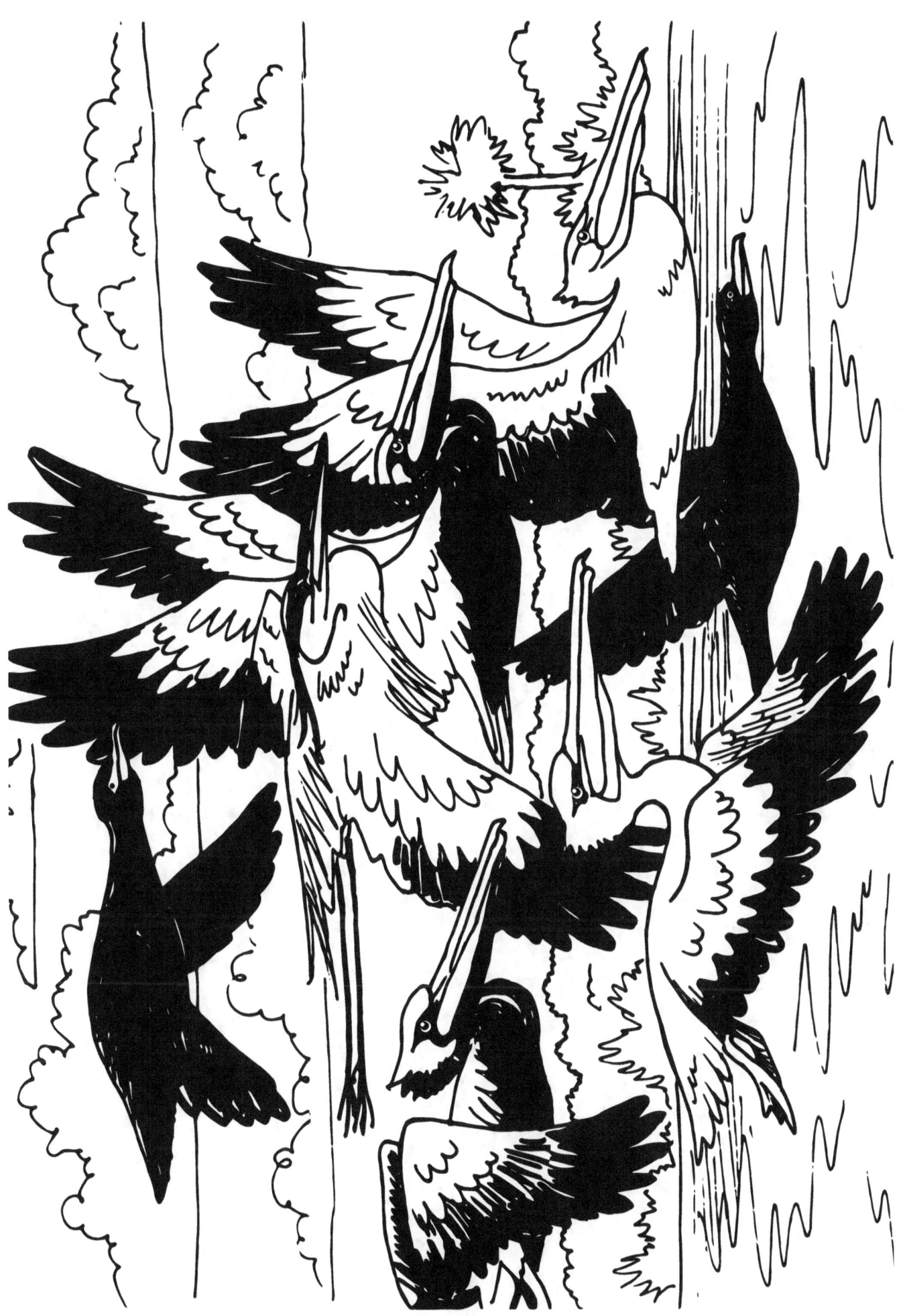

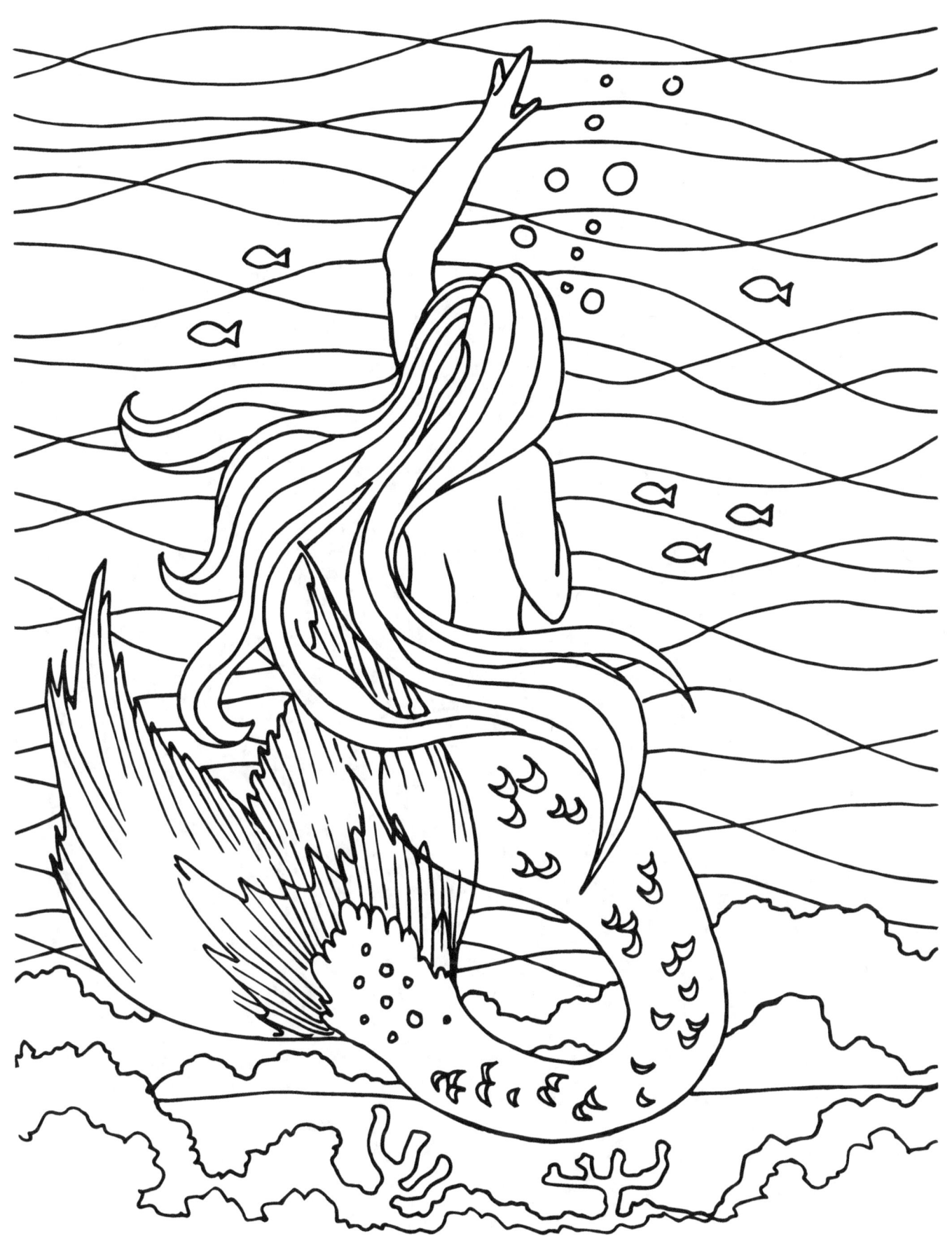

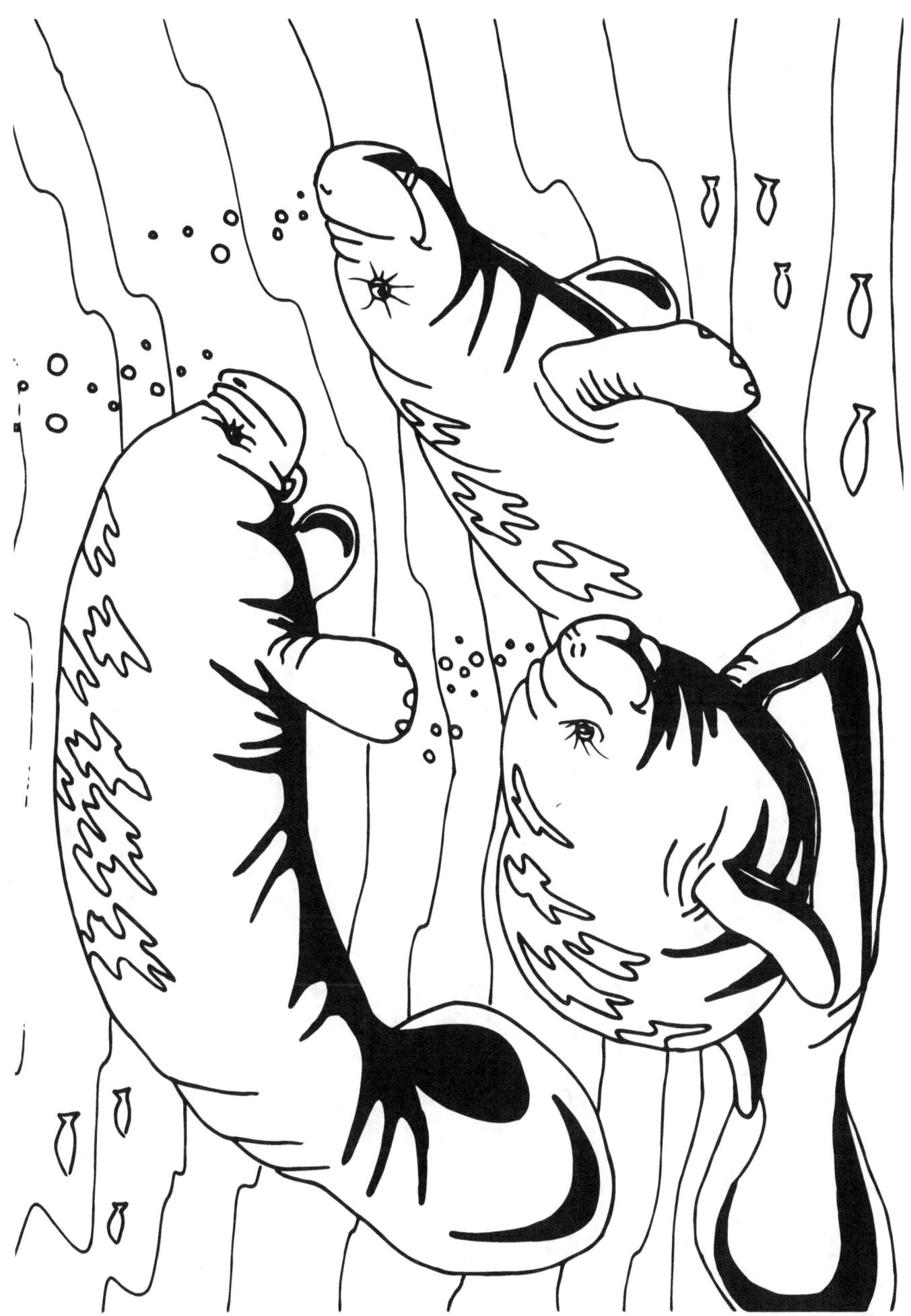

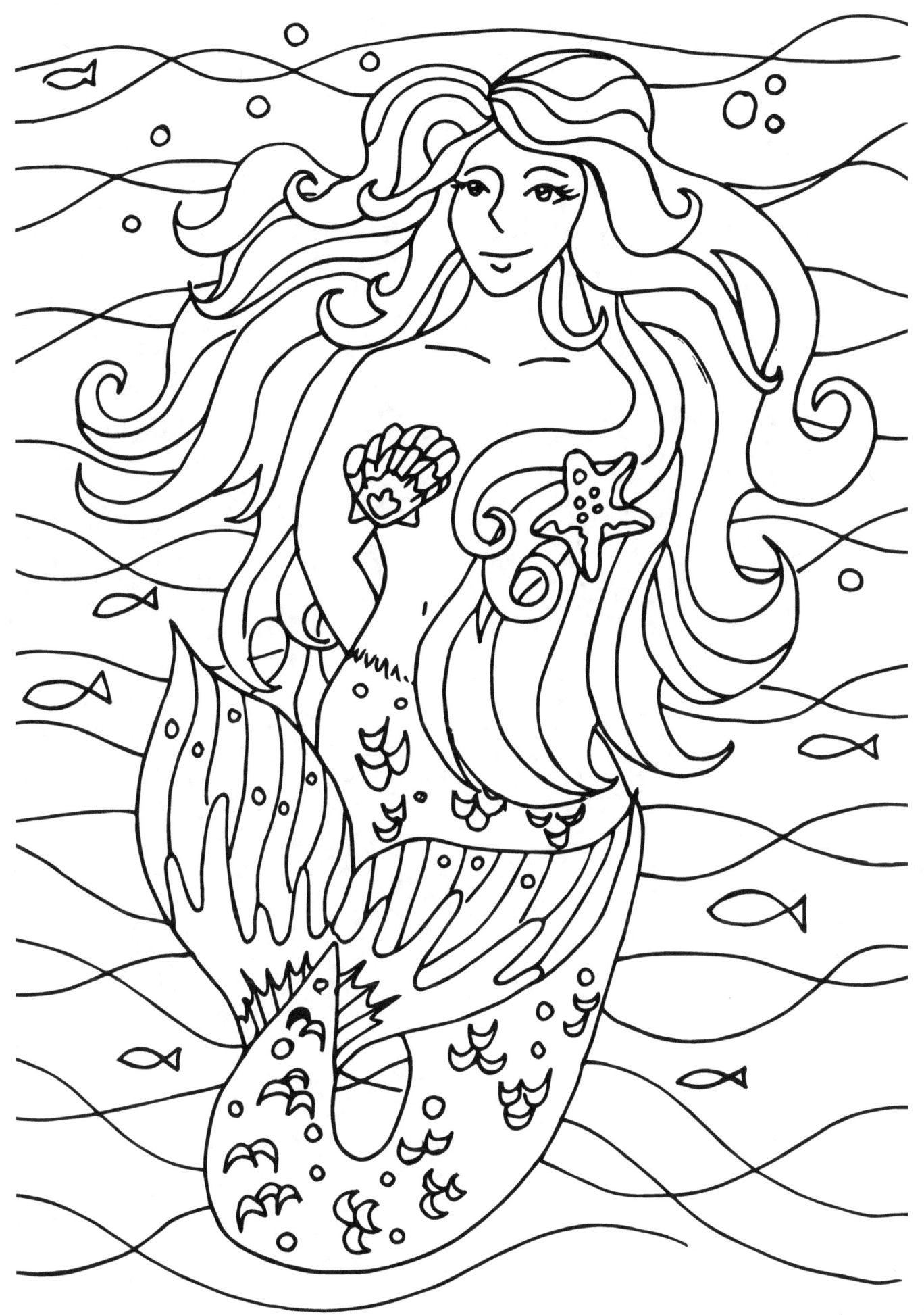

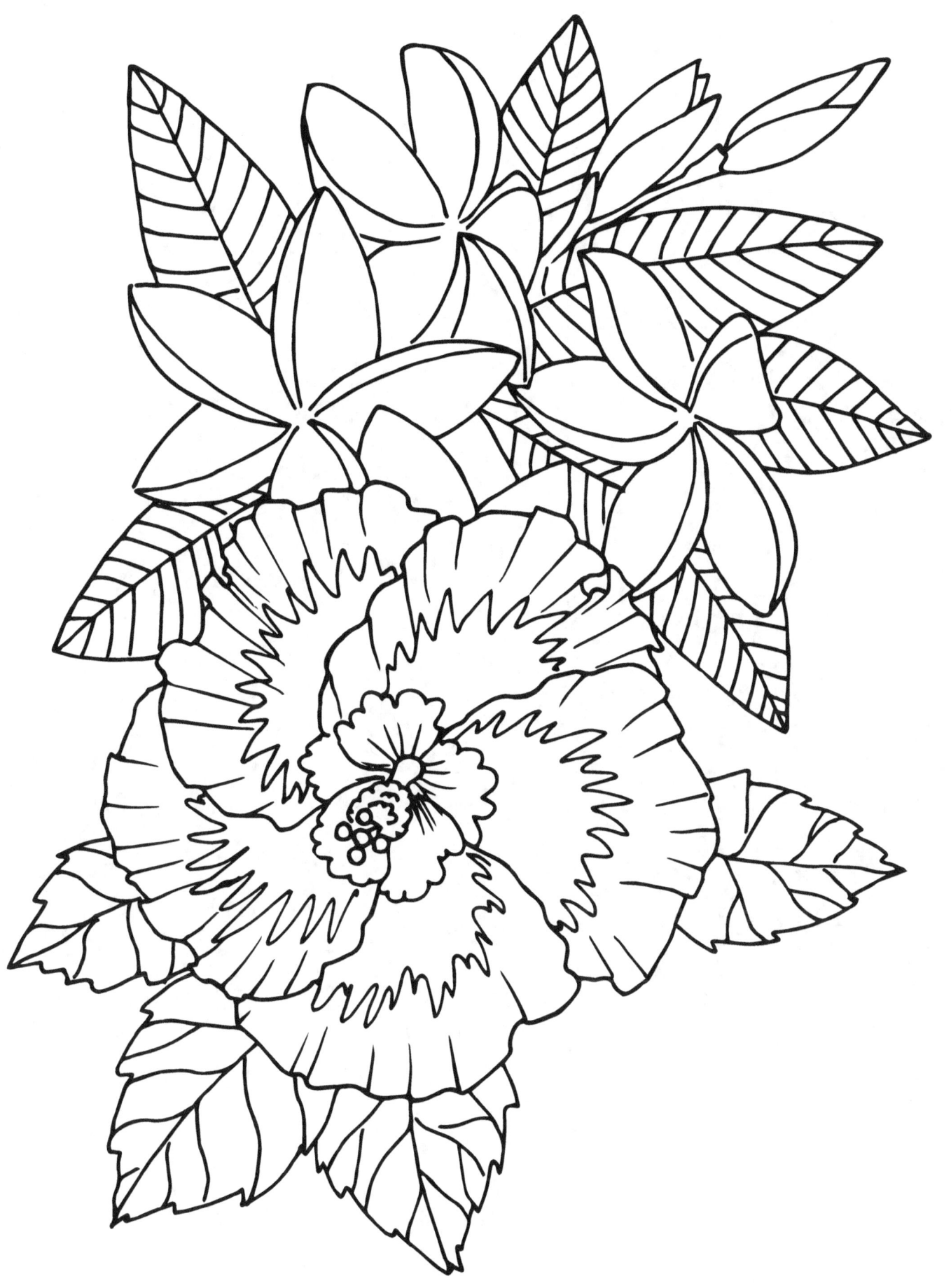

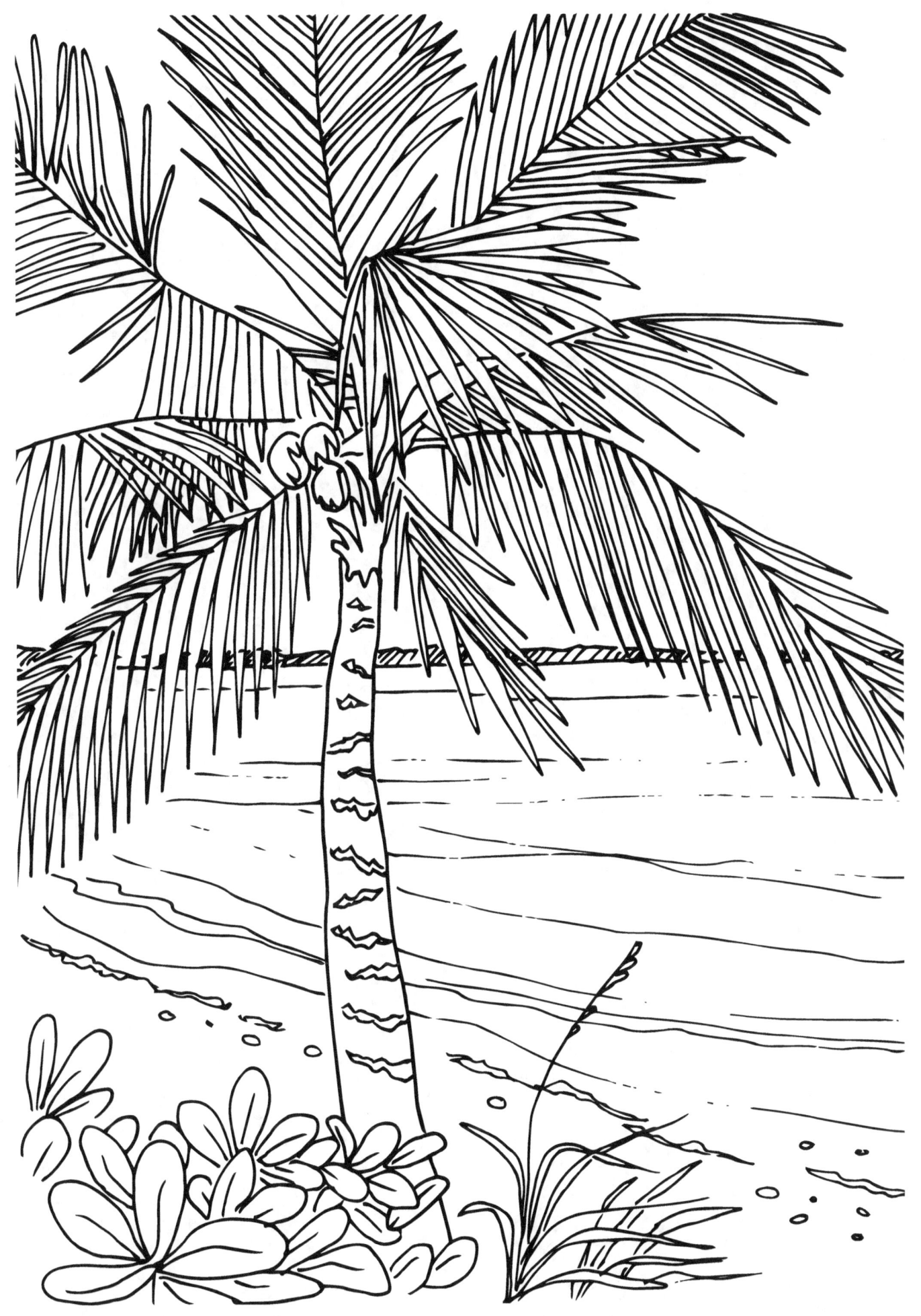